BECAUSE IT IS

KENNETH PATCHEN was born December 13, 1911, in Niles, Ohio, and educated at the Alexander Meiklejohn Experimental College of the University of Wisconsin. As a young man, he worked in a steel mill and held many other types of jobs, but after receiving a Guggenheim fellowship for a first book of verse, *Before the Brave* (1936), he has devoted himself to poetry, prose, and painting. Many of his works have been translated and published abroad; to date he has done more than 500 volumes in his "Painted Books" series.

In 1957 Patchen pioneered in the "public birth of Poetry-Jazz" by reading his poems to the accompaniment of the well-known Chamber Jazz Sextet in nightclubs and concert halls on the West Coast, breaking attendance records in San Francisco and Los Angeles. He went on to read successfully in the East and has also recorded his poetry under Cadence and Folkway labels. The poet's first play, "Don't Look Now," has been produced in Palo Alto, California, by the Troupe Theater, and off-Broadway in New York City.

Patchen has lived in New York, Boston, Santa Fe, Phoenix, New Orleans, and Connecticut; he is married and currently resides on the California coast.

He was one of five long-established poets to be honored by the National Foundation on the Arts and the Humanities with a special award of $10,000 in recognition of his "lifelong contribution to American letters."

In his fifty-seventh year Patchen published his *Collected Poems* drawn from the contents of twelve of his most important books.

BY KENNETH PATCHEN

Aflame and Afun of Walking Faces
An Astonished Eye Looks Out Of The Air
A Sheaf of Early Poems
A Surprise For The Bagpipe-Player
Because It Is
Before The Brave
But Even So
Cloth Of The Tempest
Doubleheader
Fables & Other Little Tales
First Will & Testament
Glory Never Guesses
Hallelujah Anyway
Hurrah For Anything
Memoirs Of A Shy Pornographer
Orchards, Thrones & Caravans
Out of the World of Patchen
Panels For The Walls Of Heaven
Pictures Of Life And Of Death
Poemscapes
Poems Of Humor & Protest
Red Wine & Yellow Hair
See You In The Morning
Selected Poems
Sleepers Awake
The Collected Poems of Kenneth Patchen
The Dark Kingdom
The Famous Boating Party
The Journal Of Albion Moonlight
The Love Poems of Kenneth Patchen
The Teeth Of The Lion
They Keep Riding Down All The Time
To Say If You Love Someone
Translations from the English
When We Were Here Together
Wonderings

BECAUSE IT IS

Poems and Drawings by

KENNETH PATCHEN

A NEW DIRECTIONS PAPERBOOK

FOR MIRIAM

CONTENTS

BECAUSE IT IS

BECAUSE *TO UNDERSTAND*
ONE MUST BEGIN SOMEWHERE

John Edgar Dawdle married a little chicken
And went to live in a hatbox
Which stood near the castlewall; but
At five o'clock the king came and
Wanted to give them a thousand buttered Rolls-Royces,
Eighty barrels of turpentine-mellowed trout, a flute
Which he claimed had belonged to a W. R. Mozart,
And half a glass of rounded ale.
So, not wishing to appear rude or ungrateful,
They restrung his tennis racket, subscribed to
All his magazines, and each wrote PEACE
On his behind; for he'd hurried over
Without bothering to dress. Oh, he was fine!
And they all stayed there . . . except him,
And Dawdle, and the pretty little chicken.

BECAUSE *THEY WERE*
VERY POOR THAT WINTER

The only mother he could afford was a skinny old man
Who sat on the roof all day drinking champagne—
(The real stuff of course was much too expensive);
Previous to that, about a year later,
She joined the Society For The Placating
Of Polar Giraffes—and almost immediately discovered
That by earnestly pronouncing "Your coat's wet"
In Arabic, great numbers of drowned sailors
Would drop from the sky and dance
Through the streets until shot by cops.
So, being just turned three, little Coralou
Naturally bristled at her grandfather's suggestion that
They go together to the stationhouse and
Try the new lavatory facilities there. "Conscientious taxpayer,
Are you!" she snorted. "I suppose that's why you've
Got your overcoat pockets stuffed with snapshots
Of Martha Washington playing basketball on rollerskates!"
Obscure indeed are the vestments of destiny:
In the end, rose and ostrich smell much
Alike; and only the thinking of clouds
Keeps the world on its untroubled course.

BECAUSE *SHE FELT*
BASHFUL WITH PALM TREES

His father decided to rent a car
That had belonged to an old Gypsy;
And, in order to avert the risk,
Particularly in alleys and on enclosed bridges,
Of mustache-entanglement, to drive it backwards
Across the country. But when they opened
The trunk compartment, expecting to find there
A supply of used burro-stoppers—those
Staples of the Mexican stage—without which,
They had been cautioned, no Presidential audience
Could be in the completest sense satisfactory;
They were a little disappointed to find
Only a great blind white lion seated
On the very edge of the air.
There are days nobody gets a break.

BECAUSE *EVERYBODY* *LOOKED SO FRIENDLY I RAN*

Oh, the foxy chairabbit and the goofy beduck
They go out to buy a house of their own.
Oh, leave pretty little Melissa some, boys,
And let your golden rooster ride on Hallelujah's back
Till you perceive the weeping angel in that stone.
Oh, the spotless stovelephant and the grimy dishclothclown
They have gone to give their precious little damn about
The why and the wonder of the world; you do the same, boys!
Oh, lay it on the water, lean it on the wind;
We ain't got long, boys—it's about time we begin!
Oh, the kind of angel I'm on the side of
Won't ever try to hide from the terrible responsibilities of love!

BECAUSE *THE ZEBRA-PLANT BORE SPOTTED CUBS*

He grabbed the beanpot off the clothesline
And poured hot maple syrup into his parade sneakers;
And still it was a mess! (Hear footnote above.)—
Like frantic horsemen trying to exchange nightgowns on a lake.
"Today," announced the kindlingwood, "September begins."
And the sinkstopper growled: "Wha-at! on April 10th!"
"It is a mite late this year," admitted a swansnail,
Ruffling up its shell and trying ineffectually to scowl.
"Shut up!" commanded Grover Clevewater Giraffe. "Let's
Everybody get on this here blade of grass;
Then the one with the handsomest neck will
Be given all the jellybuns. How's that?"
The old philosopher slowly lowered his stone:
"Suppose," he said, "you were a wisp of sour loneliness
Stuck to the wrong side of a life; would you right away
Have someone locked up for trying to lap your hand?
Someone, that is, who had spent thirty-five years
Pasting vile-tasting labels on cans in
A dog-meat factory. Yes, they say there are rooms;
That there are reasons; that things make sense . . . Yes, woof! woof!
But it will all come right; yes, it will end.
The last cruel wag to a cruel tale.
Ah, no . . . life is not a story that children
Should ever be allowed to hear about."

11

BECAUSE *ALL THE FORESTS*
WERE PLAYING LEAFROG

I broke a corner off the house
And put an eagle egg on it; also
I took a pretty lilacat out. But
The Captain, the Captain's wrongsidein eyewhiskers,
Her shell-tan nightgown, and the Captain's
Lightbulbous nose, as well as the Captain's back sideyard,
Now caked with ticking birds and chambermaids
Grousing about yacht prices—all these, and
A minus-fifteen policemen; an agnostic mantis;
The first cousin of a backward but capital woC—
Little Wooly, their mixed-up and sheepish skoffring;
A dead steamshovel; Miss Mildred's dyeing gear, with
Special elixirs for those without hair, as well as baldies;
Together with a weaselark; a spoonful of extremely cool
Hot saucer solos; some rubbernails; and a full trapdoor
Guarded over by an unarmed honeysuckle bush—
All these were waiting for the train. What in hell are
You doing? What are you waiting for!

BECAUSE *I DIDN'T*
MEAN NO HARM, MISTER

They chased me off and it was
Getting lonesome and I couldn't recollect anything
Much except riding with an old battered Indian
Up to the fifth floor of an empty building
And being sort of surprised when he took a pheasant sandwich
Out of his very hip pocket and lent it to some fellows.
Another time I got locked in overnight in
A shoestore, I noticed a large big grasshopper
Came in pushing a shiny cartful of wheels;
But my mother was away visiting father,
And when neither of them got home for supper,
They just stretched out in a ditch.
"To melt thin syrup you need either
A smart fire or a pretty hairy wrist."—
That was the motto of our town 'paper,
But when I couldn't get work nobody ever caught
The editor giving up any of his liberal illmannerisms.
In this country it's still as easy for a worm
To turn into a bird as for a poor boy
To wish he had some wealth or money.

BECAUSE *THE STREET SAT THERE SCRATCHING HIMSELF*

I wanted to get a lion on the hat
So I placed the first wagon one full slice
From the end of the loaf; the boatshaft,
Counterpane, tapered drum, and the baggy climate,
I carefully wove into ridges, and the resulting stair
Into corners of fox and flax and gleaming satchel tacks.
Trees' hair . . . ribboning weave of birds . . . summer has
Some pretty fetching tricks up her sleeve. And up there—
Ah! you far out crazy daisies! It'll take some real circling
To square that field with any unified theory! UFO
And I'll PDQ (Provide the Dogstar Quills). In general,
Everything is unfathomably particular. Air has
Firmer bones than any beast, fish, or unheritable blossom.
Memory does leave strange lions on our hats . . .
When I worked in the Haggerstown quarry
The mules had red whiskers down to their knees;
Now the willows kneel glumly on the riverbank,
And no carts call, no cook's gong startles the squid.
Who remembers the timid house on Duggers Lane?
The only one for marvels around without
Roof, walls, doors, windows, tenants, or rooms.
Oh, who remembers Old Bob, the blind taxi driver?
Does anyone even remember what the near-sighted Eskimo said
When he came upon a shivering angel in a snowdrift?
Who today remembers Miss Mammy Tina? or Little Ragged Jeffie?

16

—And the showwindow of the taxidermist's just off Lubbert Alley,
Where, for seventeen motionless years, she held him on her lap?
No, alas . . . most of us have to keep pretty hopping and headsup
Just so as how our hats don't go slipping off under some cuspidacious bus.

17

BECAUSE *WE MAKE OUT WHEN WE'RE IN*

Most of his kinsfolk were related but
The druggist's sister would get hold
Of somebody she'd bend that person
The shape of a piece of lampwick
And tie him maybe ten feet or so
Off the ground right in the deepest
Part of the lake and you'd ask her
Why she did it, she'd always say
Tomorrow I'll take him to see
My lawyer if he likes; another boy
We knew at that time—a sort
Of nervous type named Ebbret,
Who, afraid of rabbits, went round
Disguised as a prickly carrot . . .
He was later eaten by a horse in Arizona—
Should also be mentioned here,
If only for the reason that his mother,
And his grandmother, and his great-grandmother,
Were all so ticklish that not only
Did they never marry, but it was worth
The arm of many an unsuspecting stranger
Just to venture a polite handshake with them
On the steps of the half-gutted townhall.

BECAUSE *THE FLYBYNIGHT* *PEERED INTO THE WASHTUB*

Poor Clerinda Soup sat on in Roanoke,
But they all quickly left again anyhow.
While drenched cyclists hung by their toes,
White panthers came from the wings bearing
In some cases feathers and in wooden jars
The prettily shingled songs of barnowls. Never
Were they happier than when I strolled
Into that hotel room only to find myself
And Clerinda floating past the open window;
Yet that half-quart keg containing fifty gallons
Of spiked Old Tigersnot had to be emptied twice
Before we could even get out of the world!
Oh, flaming pig in a frockcoat, blue mule with wings—
And we are but the shadows of still more shadowy things.

BECAUSE *SOMETIMES*
YOU CAN'T ALWAYS BE SO

I never read of any enforceable regulation
Against removing orangeskins from apples in private;
But when my brother tried to buy
A sandwich in the Lodi post office yesterday,
One of the town's leading social blights
Bit him in the leg! Why, only last
Week an aunt of mine had a horse
Named Sesroh fall asleep on her shoulder
In the subway! The fifth Friday in July
A flagload of my cousins were arrested for pulling
A rowboat down the main drag in Yonkers—
Despite the fact it had cost them sixty bucks
To get the governor's grandmother drunk enough
To ride nude in it! Talk about patriotism!—
Is civic mindedness to be an empty catchsword
For every schoolboy to sneak his first shave with?
Are the hallowed drawers of our forefathers to be bulged
Thus shamelessly forth above every pawnshop in the land?
I believe it was Old Mother Frietchie who said:
"Shoot, son, even if I could dance,
There are a lot better ways to have a ball
Than scraping the hair off your own head."

BECAUSE A DOOR
IN THE HILL OPENED

An old man floated through the window
And landed in my soup. Before I
Could lift him out I noticed a
Small elephant seated on his head. But it
Wasn't until I had them comfortably settled
Before the fire that still another passenger
Revealed himself: a certain page-in-waiting
To the bookish Lady Tougai of Beddingham-on-Aiggs,
Who, while still a child, kept poor Roger Overnott
Waiting forty-nine years on the sunken balcony
Above the potting salon—an incident which
Led to the rather heated founding of Antzpantts
Near Blisterbotham (the township of pretty Dade County,
Where, as everyone knows, the repeating rifle
Was first introduced to a joyous populace
On Christmas Day, 1847.) "Tell me, sir," I said,
Hoping to ascertain whether I had to deal
With injury or simple affectation, for the old man
Kept clapping his hand to the seat of his pants;
"Is anything amiss?" To which he answered:
"A miss? Hell no, it's my wife—she insists on
Keeping her damn snapping turtles in my back pocket!"

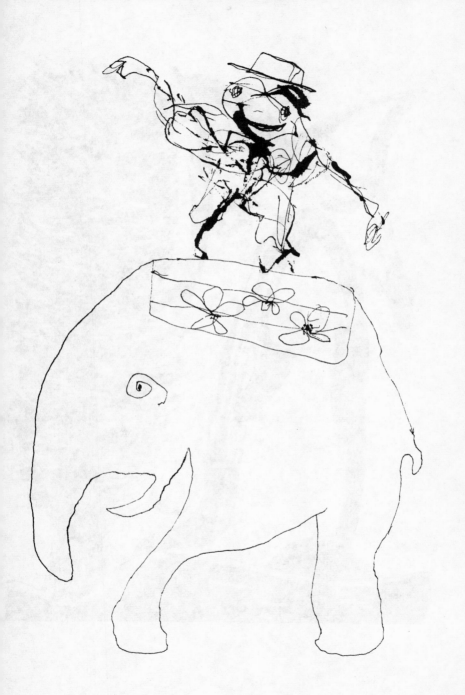

BECAUSE *A FIRTREE*
SHOOK HANDS WITH ORION

That famous Irish constellation, my birth-badge,
Only higher than my Scotch-kited grandfather at his
Melancholicly rollicking best; they felt it time
I learned from him about McKevin's curse,
And why the Countess had her belly
Painted that day beside the Cambrian Sea.
But first, since I was only six,
And of wayward temper, they took me
By a roundabout route to the meatbutcher's,
Where, between hands of Pilatatti, my cousins
Taught meditation, wig-powdering, and the several
Systems for preventing rain from falling upward;
As well as explaining—when they were
Of a mind to, which was never—
Why Mellifenza Galt Mertin refused to comment
When the milkman climbed into her bathtub.
But soon, purloined by a very curious tribe
Of Indians, we were escorted to Seattle, Maryland,
Then a missionary wickiup below Lake Friedrichskul—
And so I never saw grandfather, cousins, or myself again.

BECAUSE *GOING NOWHERE* *TAKES A LONG TIME*

Something in the climate of a hammer
Struck him when young. Call a
Sparrow a lamp, you'll still need
The liking of chairs to settle
What is at bottom only painted over
Cloth; and that flat cunning of plates,
How little it speaks above the soup's
So roundly directional bravura. Count the sky
A pan, you'll still be hard put to find
Any flash in its like. But ah, alas, alas,
Lottipo . . . the mushy marshes, those tree-lined woods,
The so-small journeying, and the trivial occupants thereof . . .
These, too, and all else, alas, are only real. So may we
Remember once again how the grasses cause the wind to move . . .
Ah, alas, dear Toppilo, what then is this realm that seems
So like a cell, without jailor or judge, or witness even . . .?
And that we love! is this not a proof of something!
No, I admit—not necessarily of heaven . . .

BECAUSE *THE GROUND-CREATURE* *LOOKED SO SAD*

The little green blackbird watched a sunflower
And a child's swing and an old woman crying.
So the tiger asked him if he'd seen
The little green blackbird around anywhere.
The tiger was there too, and also
A tiger just in from the forest.
Well, the little green blackbird also watched
A willow tree's birth and a winged crocodile too.
So then the lion asked him if he'd seen
The little green blackbird around anywhere.
You see, the lion was there too, and also
A huge bearded mouse that looked like a lion,
But was really a fat brown fish too lazy to shave;
In those days, only the most timid barbers took along
Their razors when they went in swimming.
But the little green blackbird felt pretty good
And he got himself a cuckoo named Willie Watt,
A baby whale named Willie Watt, and a big yeller hound dog
Which everyone called Willie Watt, but whose name
Was really Willie Watt; in those days, nobody minded.
So the flea's sister asked him if he'd seen
The little green blackbird around anywhere.

The flea's wife was there too, and also
An uncle of the flea's cousin's sister,
Who was also Willie Watt's father. You see, in those days,
Nobody minded and it was pretty nice.

31

BECASUE *THE BOY-HEADED LARK PLAYED ONE*

The little green blackbird became quite anxious
To try the little-known guitar-trombone-ophone
For himself; however, before having a go at it,
He went up into the Great Smoky Mountains
And there meditated eleven years with nothing
To eat or drink except a variety of foods
And beverages. Then, one evening toward night,
It suddenly came to him to wonder
Why the sky was up above there; and also,
Whether, if he could stand on top of it,
The sky might not wonder the same thing about him.
So he ran lickity-split down the mountain
And told an old fellow on a bike about
His idea: (Of course at the time he didn't know
That the bulgy-legged old fellow was a train robber,
But when he got home his was gone . . . and only a few
Wisps of stale steam still clung round the cabin door.)
"Alas," said the little green blackbird sadly;
"I always thought it just another futility of speech,

32

That 'train of thought' thing. Oh well, I'll drop by
The Nightingale Café; perhaps Dolly and Kate and the Captain
Will be back from their wedding. Now, let me see . . .
'Accumulation' is a long word; and 'candles'
Is another, though its length is more variable."

BECAUSE *MY HANDS HEAR* *THE FLOWERS THINKING*

I scooped up the moon's footprints but
The ground climbed past with a sky
And a dove and a bent vapor.
The other half of cling together wove by
In the breath of the willows; fall in
Sang eagle ox ferret and emerald arch.
O we, too, must learn to live here;
To use what we are. O fall in now!
For only love is community! Of various likenesses, none
Unless one love! In the lionleaf, the sonshade
Spreading over a father's road! When we love,
God thinks in us. And in that home-going time,
We see with the eyes of grass; and in the trees
Hear our own voices speak! So gently, gently, I say
That sleep is the secret-releasing key to this world.
Our lives are watching us—*but not from earth.*

BECAUSE *SUNSET CAME*
AT HALF-PAST NOON

A spirited bookkeeper went to the courthouse
And, using a special paper, drew up
Warrants for the arrest and immediate apprehension
Of everyone in power . . . anywhere, anytime, for
Any and all reasons—including his own;
These noble, honorable, forthright, all-sacrificing individuals
Were then sealed in a leadcoated envelope
And rocketed up as a Christmas message.
Shortly after a bearded hand with several fingers
Bitten off at the knuckle drifted down.

BECAUSE *HIS SISTER SAW* *SHAKESPEARE IN THE MOON*

The little green blackbird decided to study
Some history and geography; now, this meant going
To places like Portugal and Ayr Moor Gullibaad;
So he had some cards printed and
Handed them out. This of course started
A war, because the cards were printed
With ink. And the little green blackbird
Arrived in Portugal not only without cards,
But without a head, or arms, or legs,
Or even a little toe. This might not have been
So bad had he been feeling all right.
And it was no better in Ayr Moor Gullireet either;
In fact, it was just as sad really. "So much
For history and geography," he reflected
Ruefully; "but at least I'm a lot luckier
Than those poor unfortunates who still have heads
Left to think about what's going to happen to them."

BECAUSE *HE KEPT IMAGINING*
A PENSIVE RABBIT

The little green blackbird went off outdoors
And sat on a tree under a spreading chair.
When the sun came out it got dark
But the little green blackbird hadn't ever
Felt that lonely before and he laughed.
So some dinnerplates broke, the sun awoke,
The waitress in her flowered apron spoke;
And the little green blackbird sadly answered:
"If a friend of mine comes inquiring for me,
Tell him I've gone to join my grief
To the wintry crying of the northern sea."
And he leaned back with a puzzled smile,
Like the tiger amused by a sundial.
So the door closed, the rain closed,
The sun closed; also, the moon, a jar
Of raisin pudding, the tenth of January,
And half a raccoon. Now, alas, there was
Nothing left except the world; and nobody
In his right mind expects the world
To do anything now except close.

BECAUSE *HIS OTHER DOG*
WAS A HORSE

The kettlemaker's mother removed the bin but
Took away the bench; nevertheless, their son turned
Up under a field of swaying quiffpots
Who were trying to dry water on a cold fire.
The result was she married with her worst foot
Under the pillow, as the country people would say;
But do you think England, or Ecuador, or Sumatra,
Or even the so-called Friendly Islands where Mead,
Mook, and Tizzle wrote their memorable paper
On the significance of the coconut and the ripe banana
As referents in the erogenous conditioning of primitives;
Or even the judiciously considerate Solomon Group
Where Old Smiley Sigmund looked for a bloody boar
In the rushes and mistook his own reflection
For a dimpled little Moses, complete with long gray beard
And a frown to curdle the milk of a stone Madonna—
Do you think any of these even winced when they busted
Everything in her house that so much as hinted
That it had been made for any other reason
Than that it was cheap, and vicious, and of consummate hideousness?
If you do, I can't imagine how they'll ever be able to tell
When the moment comes to bury you.—But back to Genevieve:
She's found a really beautiful place to live;

And if you go there any time except Sunday or a weekday,
She'll be glad to show you—for the small price of your soul—
The very glove she caught the star you claim to be looking for in.

BECAUSE *HE WAS*
THINKING OF A BUMBLEBEE

The shoveltracker tossed the sand off again;
But the wormwood hare would not move.
Beside him lay the corpse of one
Named Zippity Jock, who had been hanged
For using chopsticks instead of buttonhooks
On a skittish customer in an East St. Louis
Corset fitter's shop; while above and below,
In the dried out shadow of the watertower,
Along the seams of Nellie Foophenjelly's sleepingbag,
On the tense knees and thumbs of fieldmice,
Inside the horns of odorously meditative cows,
Yes, and even under the frontporch swingamahickies
Of more than one roofed and glass-windowed house,
A small, goodnatured wind was beginning to blow.
Yet the shoveltracker went on with his work;
Interruptions meant nothing to him, or to his mother,
Whose hobby was giving imitations of a chicken swimming
On the tops of buses; nothing, nobody, could distract him!
At one point, a friendly bear with a disheveled, inky look
Sauntered up with the proposal that they mosey in to town
And tear up some lampposts together; another time,
A little man leading a kilted rhinoceros laden with shavingmugs
Offered him a part interest in The Pygmy Chamber Pot Company;

44

—Woops! he's struck water! And what's this he's lifting out?
Uh-ha! a half-drowned old hen with a pair of reading glasses
On her nose . . . and a mess of transfers stuck into her long gray feathers!

BECAUSE *HIS FRIEND CLAIMED*
THERE WEREN'T ANY

The little green blackbird ran on and on
Until he chanced to meet a little green blackbird.
But the little green blackbird couldn't get
His car to work and so he said,
"Will you come to my house at seven?
Mike and Ellie are there right now;
However, if they don't show up, Joe Bill
Has promised to rub fresh mud into
Our shirts over behind the new schoolhouse."
"And what will that cost us?" asked
The little green blackbird, adjusting his thumbs.
"Only fifty apiece," answered the little green blackbird.
"Besides, I'm not so sure I like your attitude!
Obviously you're drunk. Here, help me up."
So the little green blackbird drove off
Down the road until he reached a bridge;
Then, adjusting his cap, and his thumbs,
He said, "What are you doing in that river?"
And the little green blackbird replied sharply,
"Waiting for Joe Bill's sister, that's what!
She comes here every Tuesday to wash his shirt."
"But this is Tuesday," the little green blackbird
Snorted, pausing to adjust his parade hat,
His honey-bee-striped hip-length socks,

His bright red paper wading boots, and
His well-worn thumbs; "You must be drunker
Than I thought!" And he drove into the lake.

BECAUSE *IT'S GOOD*
TO KEEP THINGS STRAIGHT

Now the little green blackbird liked a mouse
And a Malayan sunbear and a horse
And a beetle and a mouse and a horse
And a mouse and a leopard and a beaver
And a black fox and a fox squirrel and a lion
And a buffalo and a beaver and a donkey
And a tiger and a gorilla and a panther
And a salamander and a periwinkle and an ox
And an elephant and an alligator and an armadillo
And a mouse and a mule and a beetle
And a moonfish and a buffalo and a snail
And a horse and a lion and a butterfly
And a horse and a tiger and a mouse;
And the leopard and the donkey and the horse
And the buffalo and the ox and the elephant
And the mouse and the beetle and the gorilla
And the horse and the periwinkle and the mouse
And the panther and the lion and the tiger
And the butterfly and the beaver and the snail
Also liked the little green blackbird;
But the horse and the armadillo and the lion
And the buffalo were quite indifferent to him;
While the beetle and the mouse and the moonfish

And the salamander and the mule and the beaver
Didn't care one way or the other about him;
Whereas the mouse and the horse and the mouse
And the tiger didn't even know he existed.

BECAUSE GROWING A MUSTACHE WAS PRETTY TIRING

The little green blackbird's father always said:
"A bear and a bean and a bee in bed,
Only on Bogoslof Island can one still get
That good old-fashioned white brown bread!" This made a
Very deep impression on the little green blackbird,
So he decided to forget the whole thing.
But first he painted a stolen motorcycle on the sidewalk
And sold it to a nearsighted policeman.
By then of course the little green blackbird
Remembered that his father also did impressions
Of J. Greenstripe Whittier on freshly-painted parkbenches.
So he invited nineteen hundred rabbits over for dinner;
And they each brought him a tin-plated goldfish,
A handful of gloves, the drawing of a frosty breath,
And one of those decks of newfangled playing cards,
The kind that bite people. Well, when it came time
To go home, all nineteen thousand rabbits filed out
In a pregnant silence, that was broken only
By the sound of their low-pitched voices
Raised in speech. Whereupon the father
Of the little green blackbird quietly said:
"It is our sentence, to endure;
And our only crime, that we are here to serve it."

BECAUSE *ABOVE THE CLOUDS* *LITTLE FROGOOSES FLOATED*

The Countess Cherrywhite left her shoeshine stand
And hurried down to Texas; within three
Minutes the mad dentist was back: "Come,"
Said he, brandishing his drills, "it's time
For your haircut, dearie." (Actually her head
Was still bandaged from the last one;
Even her dog, her parrot, her goldfish,
Her fryingpan, and her vacuum cleaner were
Still heavily swathed in gauze; her brother
In Weehawken kept his toupee in a vault—
And his neighbors on either side carried
Sawed-off shotguns even to the dinnertable.)
"Look-it here, you!" the Countess Cherrywhite protested;
"Dey got laws dat say no boy
What's not in his right mind can
Molest innocent folks lessen he's provided wit'
De proper Christian license to snuff dem out
On a rational, scientific basis . . . at a million or two
A clip, by Gar!"—Back at the
Shoeshine stand, Thanxamilion Boruschloski,
A self-employed idler, and perennial viewer with a-charm,
Stole a cheap look at the stars,
Said in a conspiratorial whisper to a passing statesman,
"I think we'll make it all right,

52

If mothers like yours go out of business soon enough."
—And smiled broadly. (Which was no mean feat,
Since he was only three and a half tall.)

BECAUSE *THEIR BELLS*
NEVER TOLLED THE TRUTH

Oh, the duchess combs her mirrored boredom
From the whore's son elegance of her lair;
But if I had my proper choice, boys,
I'd put most of here over there.
Oh, the rich man's got his troubles,
And the poor man's got some too;
But if I had my say about it, kiddies,
I'd kindly tell them both a few.
For the world is just as lousy rotten
As people damn well want it to be.

BECAUSE *WHERE THEY PLANTED*
SKYGREEN LEOPARDS GREW

She raced along the timbers of a
Rosebud and there was a cardgame going
On and also a sorrow-rue between two
Old landladies contemplating the handiwork of
Their most out-of-head tenants—
But the party in the orchard
Was something else!—all those he-goats
Had clumb up to the bottom of
The well expecting to have their hats
Tuned, and maybe sneak a look at
The Bobbsey Twins getting booted out of
Some sportinghouse for insisting on single fares;
However, when a lumberjack with checkered spats
And waffle-proof knickers invited them to
Tea on page 287 of Catullus' *Private Capers*
Of Randolph Makepuce Emerywheel—while the piano
Temptingly played ragtime on their tossing ribs—
They were not at all surprised to hear that
Two handmaidens had just been pinched for being gloveless.

BECAUSE *THE NERVOUS VINE* *WOULDN'T TWINE*

He and they and the ladderleaner's step-niece
Charged into the forest to rub elbows;
It was still pretty soapy but not all geese
Drink wine in the summertime. "Well, Jason,"
The first soldier said, "expect a lot more
Of my kind along; we'll add a bit of real color—
Show man the pretty water that's in him; get to the core
Of his nasty little apple; brighten his pallid wool;
Give him the peace that only comes with war."
So, since that sounded completely disgusting,
They got right at it: hack, hack, hooray!
And up on Mars they damn near
Died laughing. I suppose from that distance
Caesar's backside does look about as fetching,
And kissable, as an elbow in the ground;
Whereas here, of course, it's the holiest artifact of our civilization.

BECAUSE SOMETIMES THE HANDWRITING EATS AWAY THE WALL

Oh the trash disposal unit shlupps happily
Through a stack of Mozart—as arranged for
Hi-futility Disneyphone; and the yawning deep freeze
Settles ever further into the Bloodywood bed.
A one-ah, two-ah—
O poor Charlie and Jane,
They went off on that midnight train;
While lucky Sue and Mr. Brown,
They stayed right there in the burning town.
For the star-spangled bull has swallowed the tiddlewink,
And the chrome-plated devil stirs in the kitchen sink.
So God bless the riders and the residers,
And the in- and the outsiders too;
'Cause it'll all be a lot like it is right now,
If that's left up to the likes of me and you.
For the worst and the best work together now as a team . . .
As the mushroom-hungry devil strides through that valley so green.
Yeah! the Loonies! the Loonies are really loose!
And it's much, much later and lousier than anybody thinks!

BECAUSE *THE SMALL MAN WAS A STRANGER*

The friendly **greeting chicken** said, "Will you
Join me in a dish of **sleepy grapes**?"
"If you're quite sure there'll be room
For both of us," the **small man** replied.
"It's been so long since I've eaten,
Something seems to fly out each time I open
My **mouth**." On the dark meat of the sky
Bright dabs of mu**star**d began to appear,
And a **moody** fol**lowing** of **crows** accompanied
Them to her door. Once safely inside
The **small man** banged his head
On a **beam** and proceeded to fall
Into a sewing basket on the **couch**.
"Hush," the **greeting chicken** said. "Oscar's asleep."
And she pointed to a tiny b**owl**
On the table. The stranger thought it
Damn odd to call a bowl Oscar.
But wanting to be polite, he said,
"Excuse me, did you say something about
Eating some grapes?" She looked at him in wonderment:
"What! after I've just got their little tails all curled,
And their pretty red bottoms tucked in for the night!
Come, Oscar—you can't trust anybody these days."
And sadly she sped away with her blinking b**owl**.

BECAUSE *MR. FLOWERS THE BOATMAN SAILED WALLS*

The Kumbria-Doggo began to sing again:
"Oh, they got up and sat so quietly,
All the dead who do not speak;
Though oak leaves grow on the oak,
And now and then a mouse does squeak."
Sam asked a riddle which none could doubt:
"If psalter and scepter season Caesar's broth,
What's the weight of a dead bird's thought?"
To which Bess, his nicest of kin, replied:
"As well a sea without looking as
Maid without your doing! O merry me,
And I shall smack plum in mysteries be!"
But the Boatman paid no mind, not he;
For wisdom is its own price in such peaceful company.

BECAUSE *THE WHOLE WORLD*
WAS ON FIRE

A little owlion named Tom Birkis Jonnes
And a shy gorillapple named Miss Hazel Hurryweather
Raced like mad all the way to the moviehouse
But it was some corny picture about these
Crooks riding on a train and an
Old woman keeps getting drunk so the
Ski troopers search everybody and just
At the border who should appear but
Twelve guys with hair on the outside
Of their hats and they don't even
Have a chance to start dealing when
A big dog in a jellyglass face suddenly
Comes on deck and machineguns the audience;
So Tom Birkis Jonnes and Miss Hazel Hurryweather
Were certainly glad they'd gone to the woods instead—
For there they met many nice friends and
Had much good talk and after a while
Got married and ate supper and some delicious pies.

BECAUSE *TODAY'S MONKEY*
MAY WELL BE TOMORROW'S TUESLOCK

I carted the steeple-knocker over there,
And I nailed another egg about here.
There seemed to be a horse waving
About four feet above Chicago, but damn
Little doing around Linwood. For one thing,
The disinterest rates were so out of line that
Of all my nine brothers only one
Was born with shoes on; and he
Had to fill out several tricky questionnaires
Before his first powder was even dry.
Small wonder my Uncle "Auntie Boo" Bludwater
Always said if they'd let everybody ride
Free on Lincoln's birthday you'd soon put
A stop to razorblade advertising on passenger trains.

68

BECAUSE *THERE ARE*
ROSES, SWANS AND HERBUGAZELLES

The lanterneater's daughter went to a banquet
Dressed as the phone number of an elm tree;
And they placed some angry bottles in array,
Set twelve runners to making boot soup—
Now don't shove me! interrupted Sam Bluesnow—as
The sideboard stifled a yawn; but the booths
Of the cuttlefishthieves and the short-wheeled carts
Of the pigmypigvendors took off like burning shirts.
(A word about screens: flies. Even in Skymirrortown
People got legs like U, only they're upside down.)
Oh, the lanterneater's daughter she sits all alone;
Not much she can do to stop what's been done.
For the leaves they fall on the moving water,
And the wedding guests are all dead and gone.
Oh, winter's chill dust will blight every green—
And Sam may cry but Sam will die.

BECAUSE *IN THIS*
SORROWING STATUE OF FLESH

They were hopeful of a curtain raiser
That would not sputter off in walls
And worklands instinct with shadows before gates
Where all helmets and orders eventually collect;
But none went to himself fully or
Made his might little enough to bear
The green loaves in his hand of leaves.
"All memory is piecemeal murder;
The hater in the mirror, it has a mother's impersonal gaze . . ."
"I do not think of the shorelights blurring out,
Or of the gray and raging glee
That slates these waves; but only
Of her tiny delicacy, of the strange gentleness of her fingers . . .
And of how very odd it is
That my man's heart should now be torn right out of me!"
"But the event itself, it has no speech; nor has it
Any meaning or purpose outside its own being. For existence
Is an animal substance, indivisible, and hence, unknowable;
And all things—stars, brides, and apple boughs—
And non-things, too—such as "history's happenings"—
Are but its cells and bones and tissues."
"And the voice of the father, there is no mercy in it;
All that vast chemistry of the sun . . . and little birds freeze!"
"I do not now think so much of what may only be idly argued;
For it seems a fact still of some importance, that I am dying."

72

BECAUSE *IT DIDN'T*
LIKE THE STORY ANYWAY

I stuffed the letter behind the pumphandle
And instructed the judge: you must choose
Between flashing about in trolleycars, both to
Left and just arrived, and making a
Silly basketlunch of yourself everytime some
Otter decides he bonny well won't. The neck
Of a floor loomed above the enwraptured lovers;
A cluster of peels appeared, seeking their
Friendly, nomad fruit; and Doctor Miransoli, dapper
As a noose, clumped lackadaisically into a field
But didn't pick any. Old Boy Blue
Up there, he don't seem to blow much
'Cept trouble; now, I ain't never been dead,
The little livin' man said; but I sure
Been double-deep in dyin' since I's born . . .
If there's anybody up there plays my tune,
They better get round to it pretty soon,
'Cause this jive 'bout some tree-foot unicorn
Don't music up no gravy on my spoon . . .
Man, them words just don't fit where I'm walkin';
How can I dig some corny waltz from some way-in horn
When all the deaths of my life are wailing at once?
And the judge said: "You know, there's something pretty fishy
About all you half-spitted Jonahs."

BECAUSE *TO REALLY PONDER*
ONE NEEDS WONDER

The moralistic Mrs. Winklemudjer called me to say
That in 1800 something an Abia Luw who
Lived on a private pension had a sort
Of table-like affair in his house
Where on a summer evening two ladies
Of the town indulged with him in dinner
And later being joined by an officer
Of the police his wife his mother together
With her youthful aunt's lover attired in folds
Of some stretchable cloth and armed with flowered bands
They all proceeded to an attic-cellar that was situated above
And slightly apart from the dwelling's other rooms
Staying there until their presence somewhat waning
They again went below bearing through physiological
Corporeality a marked resemblance to those kinds
Of group-individuals met with on cathedral balconies
At bird-watcher-watcher furtivities amongst deacon-duckers
Gallowsed-grandpa-goosers and before behind and between
Those railings of wood and temperament and plasticized steel
As we have come through mutual and understanding disparagement
To know them all too ill; at which point
A thatched roof two or three loafers from the bakery
Developed a low snore somewhere under its peak—

76

Now, as I think Homer or T. Cosfelder said:
You know, lads, the trouble with even the best story is,
It all too seldom tells what happened to us.

BECAUSE *A COW*
CHEWED OFF THE TRAINWHEELS

They abandoned their search for white coal
And walked across the Pacific on their
Hands and knees, thus avoiding unwary submarines;
However, just off Haverstraw, in a tremendous
Cave filled with chimneypots, matchsticks, and bagpipes,
They came upon a hippopotamus eating Edam cheese
And disclaiming: "I am your daughter Ricky Rudolph,
Arrived here yesterday by this morning's plane.
Go run and warn the rain, good pals; oh kindly do:
I don't want his little coat to get all wet too!"
And lo! the eyeless wind itself then said:
"There are crumbs for the birds; for the lion
In his golden sleep, such Africas
As make the-very sky to weep;
For all some tiny, secret each . . .
And they be laid beyond reach . . .
Owls, oxen, elm, yew, and keening beech . . .
But for me, alas, there's only what all men dream of . . .
Myself the realm of restlessness; the dark love
Of the waters; the sun's mask whirling through
The emptiness; the blind, doughy face grinning
Above the thinking void—where unimaginable wonder
Stirs with every breath of every living thing!
And life and God—and branch and star—and they be gone . . .
And they be gone and dead, as for all of you they will . . .

78

And I alone am left . . . I, the wind . . . and that shall be enough . . .
Oh, that shall be enough to start the wonder of the dark,
The bright deep of that pale visitor
Whose hair I move . . . I, the wind . . . the bird's messenger
From that other world where no being need ever mourn."
And lo! from the heavens stepped a Sorrowing Child,
And said: "Long ago a butterfly was murdered,
And the wound of it resounds through the flesh of the universe
Forever; nerve ends of grass and trees and stars
Have sped that tiny death beyond the compass
Of any man's heart to touch it back into place.
—Not that murder is done, but that it is!
For death itself is murder; however birds sing."
And the improbably wonderful hippopotamus
Went on smiling into its plate of cheese.

BECAUSE *EVERYBODY'S CLOCK* *KEEPS A DIFFERENT TIME*

Harney Harcole zipped downstairs just in time to
Grab hold of himself leaving by the roof;
But even then Maverna Vealle bowed her head,
Saying: "No! I shall not put it aside—
My cloak, cowl, and leg-blade, all in one!
Stop sniveling, mother! the joint is closed—
Locked, docked, jicky-pocked; besides, you've
Got enough load on right now to sink
The Maine and most of New Hampshire."
O night that nibbles . . . And darkness feeds
On the dark. The huddled figures.—Booom!
That time it was only a clock. The next, it may be the count-down.
Ten nine eight seven . . . Men birds and little fishes in the sea . . .
O where are the horsemen of light!—Booom!
The barroom, dark; the kingsroom, dark; the park, dark;
O the world and the water . . . *six five* . . .
Now have love and reason lost!—*four three* . . .
O the candlelight and the larks!—Booom!
And the ten doomed little Indians . . .
And the ten poor, doomed little Indians
Who have now become everyone on earth.

BECAUSE *HE LIKED*
TO BE AT HOME

He usually managed to be there when
He arrived. A horse, his name was
Hunry Fencewaver Walkins—he'd sometimes
Be almost too tired to make it;
Because, since he also hated being alone,
He was always on the alert to pop forth
At a full run whenever the door opened.
Then one day it happened—
He didn't get there in time!
Of course he couldn't risk opening the door—
So, panting, he just stood there in the hall—
And listened to the terrible sound of himself weeping
In that room he could never, never enter again.

83

New Directions Paperbooks

Ilangô Adigal, *Shilappadikaram.* NDP162.
Corrado Alvaro, *Revolt in Aspromonte.*
  NDP119.
Guillaume Apollinaire. *Selected Writings.*†
  NDP310.
Djuna Barnes, *Nightwood.* NDP98.
Charles Baudelaire, *Flowers of Evil.*† NDP71.
  Paris Spleen. NDP294.
Eric Bentley, *Bernard Shaw.* NDP59.
Wolfgang Borchert, *The Man Outside.* NDP319.
Jorge Luis Borges, *Labyrinths.* NDP186.
Jean-François Bory, *Once Again.* NDP256.
Paul Bowles, *The Sheltering Sky.* NDP158.
Kay Boyle, *Thirty Stories.* NDP62.
W. Bronk, *The World, the Wordless.* NDP157.
Buddha, *The Dhammapada.* NDP188.
Louis-Ferdinand Céline, *Guignol's Band.*
  NDP278.
  Journey to the End of the Night. NDP84.
Blaise Cendrars, *Selected Writings.*† NDP203.
B-c. Chatterjee, *Krishnakanta's Will.* NDP120.
Jean Cocteau, *The Holy Terrors.* NDP212.
  The Infernal Machine. NDP235.
Contemporary German Poetry.†
  (Anthology) NDP148.
Hayden Carruth, *For You.* NDP298.
Cid Corman, *Livingdying.* NDP289.
  Sun Rock Man. NDP318.
Gregory Corso, *Elegiac Feelings American.*
  NDP299.
  Long Live Man. NDP127.
  Happy Birthday of Death. NDP86.
Edward Dahlberg, *Reader.* NDP246.
  Because I Was Flesh. NDP227.
David Daiches, *Virginia Woolf.*
  (Revised) NDP96.
Osamu Dazai, *The Setting Sun.* NDP258.
Robert Duncan, *Roots and Branches.* NDP275.
  Bending the Bow. NDP255.
Richard Eberhart, *Selected Poems.* NDP198.
Russell Edson, *The Very Thing That Happens.*
  NDP137.
Wm. Empson, *7 Types of Ambiguity.* NDP204.
  Some Versions of Pastoral. NDP92.
Wm. Everson, *The Residual Years.* NDP263.
Lawrence Ferlinghetti, *Her.* NDP88.
  Back Roads to Far Places. NDP312.
  A Coney Island of the Mind. NDP74.
  The Mexican Night. NDP300.
  Routines. NDP187.
  The Secret Meaning of Things. NDP268.
  Starting from San Francisco. NDP 220.
  Tyrannus Nix?. NDP288.
  Unfair Arguments with Existence. NDP143.
Ronald Firbank, *Two Novels.* NDP128.
Dudley Fitts.
  Poems from the Greek Anthology. NDP60.
F. Scott Fitzgerald, *The Crack-up.* NDP54.
Robert Fitzgerald, *Spring Shade: Poems
  1931-1970.* NDP311.
Gustave Flaubert,
  The Dictionary of Accepted Ideas. NDP230.
M. K. Gandhi, *Gandhi on Non-Violence.*
  (ed. Thomas Merton) NDP197.
André Gide. *Dostoevsky.* NDP100.

Goethe, *Faust,* Part I.
  (MacIntyre translation) NDP70.
Albert J. Guerard, *Thomas Hardy.* NDP185.
Guillevic, *Selected Poems.* NDP279.
Henry Hatfield, *Goethe.* NDP136.
  Thomas Mann. (Revised Edition) NDP101
John Hawkes, *The Cannibal.* NDP123.
  The Lime Twig. NDP95.
  Second Skin. NDP146.
  The Beetle Leg. NDP239.
  The Innocent Party. NDP238.
  Lunar Landscapes. NDP274.
Hermann Hesse, *Siddhartha.* NDP65.
Edwin Honig, *García Lorca.* (Rev.) NDP102
Christopher Isherwood, *The Berlin Stories.*
  NDP134.
Alfred Jarry, *Ubu Roi.* NDP105.
Robinson Jeffers, *Cawdor and Medea.* NDP293.
James Joyce, *Stephen Hero.* NDP133.
Franz Kafka, *Amerika.* NDP117.
Bob Kaufman,
  Solitudes Crowded with Loneliness. NDP199.
Hugh Kenner, *Wyndham Lewis.* NDP167.
Lincoln Kirstein,
  Rhymes & More Rhymes of a Pfc. NDP202.
P. Lal, translator, *Great Sanskrit Plays.*
  NDP142.
Tommaso Landolfi,
  Gogol's Wife and Other Stories. NDP207.
Lautréamont, *Maldoror.* NDP207.
Denise Levertov, *O Taste and See.* NDP149.
  The Jacob's Ladder. NDP112.
  Relearning the Alphabet. NDP290.
  The Sorrow Dance. NDP222.
  With Eyes at the Back of Our Heads.
  NDP229.
Harry Levin, *James Joyce.* NDP87.
García Lorca, *Selected Poems.*† NDP114.
  Three Tragedies. NDP52.
  Five Plays. NDP232.
Carson McCullers, *The Member of the
  Wedding* (Playscript) NDP153.
Thomas Merton, *Selected Poems.* NDP85.
  Cables to the Ace. NDP252.
  Clement of Alexandria. Gift Ed. NDP173.
  Emblems of a Season of Fury. NDP140.
  Gandhi on Non-Violence. NDP197.
  The Geography of Lograire. NDP283.
  Original Child Bomb. NDP228.
  Raids on the Unspeakable. NDP276
  The Way of Chuang Tzu. NDP276.
  The Wisdom of the Desert. NDP295.
  Zen and the Birds of Appetite. NDP261.
Henri Michaux, *Selected Writings.*† NDP264.
Henry Miller, *The Air-Conditioned Nightmare.*
  NDP302.
  *Big Sur & The Oranges of Hieronymus
  Bosch.* NDP161.
  The Books in My Life. NDP280.
  The Colossus of Maroussi. NDP75.
  The Cosmological Eye. NDP109.
  Henry Miller on Writing. NDP151.
  The Henry Miller Reader. NDP269.
  Remember to Remember. NDP111.
  Stand Still Like the Hummingbird. NDP236
  The Time of the Assassins. NDP 115.
  The Wisdom of the Heart. NDP94.

Y. Mishima, *Death in Midsummer.* NDP215.
  Confessions of a Mask. NDP253.
Eugenio Montale, *Selected Poems.*† NDP193.
Vladimir Nabokov, *Nikolai Gogol.* NDP78.
New Directions 17. (Anthology) NDP103.
New Directions 18. (Anthology) NDP163.
New Directions 19. (Anthology) NDP214.
New Directions 20. (Anthology) NDP248.
New Directions 21. (Anthology) NDP277.
New Directions 22. (Anthology) NDP291.
New Directions 23. (Anthology) NDP315.
Charles Olson, *Selected Writings.* NDP231.
George Oppen, *The Materials.* NDP122.
  Of Being Numerous. NDP245.
  This In Which. NDP201.
Wilfred Owen, *Collected Poems.* NDP210.
Nicanor Parra,
  Poems and Antipoems.† NDP242.
Boris Pasternak, *Safe Conduct.* NDP77.
Kenneth Patchen, *Aflame and Afun of
  Walking Faces.* NDP292.
  Because It Is. NDP83.
  But Even So. NDP265.
  Collected Poems. NDP284.
  Doubleheader. NDP211.
  Hallelujah Anyway. NDP219.
  The Journal of Albion Moonlight. NDP99.
  Memoirs of a Shy Pornographer. NDP205.
  Selected Poems. NDP160.
  Sleepers Awake. NDP286.
  Wonderings. NDP320.
Octavio Paz, *Configurations.*† NDP303.
Plays for a New Theater. (Anth.) NDP216.
Ezra Pound, *ABC of Reading.* NDP89.
  Classic Noh Theatre of Japan. NDP79.
  The Confucian Odes. NDP81.
  Confucius. NDP285.
  Confucius to Cummings. (Anth) NDP126.
  Guide to Kulchur. NDP257.
  Literary Essays. NDP250.
  Love Poems of Ancient Egypt. Gift Edition.
  NDP178.
  Pound/Joyce. NDP296.
  Selected Cantos. NDP304.
  Selected Letters 1907-1941. NDP317.
  Selected Poems. NDP66
  The Spirit of Romance. NDP266.
  Translations.† (Enlarged Edition) NDP145.
Omar Pound, *Arabic and Persian Poems.*
  NDP305.
Raymond Queneau, *The Bark Tree.* NDP314.
Carl Rakosi, *Amulet.* NDP234.
Raja Rao, *Kanthapura.* NDP224.
Herbert Read, *The Green Child.* NDP208.
Jesse Reichek, *Etcetera.* NDP196.
Kenneth Rexroth, *Assays.* NDP113.
  An Autobiographical Novel. NDP281.
  Bird in the Bush. NDP80
  Collected Longer Poems. NDP309.
  Collected Shorter Poems. NDP243.
  Love and the Turning Year. NDP308.
  100 Poems from the Chinese. NDP192.
  100 Poems from the Japanese.† NDP147.

Charles Reznikoff, *By the Waters of Manhattan.*
  NDP121.
  Testimony: The United States 1885-1890.
  NDP200.
Arthur Rimbaud, *Illuminations.*† NDP56.
  Season in Hell & Drunken Boat.† NDP97.
Saikaku Ihara, *The Life of an Amorous
  Woman.* NDP270.
Jean-Paul Sartre, *Baudelaire.* NDP233.
  Nausea. NDP82.
  The Wall (Intimacy). NDP272.
Delmore Schwartz, *Selected Poems.* NDP241.
Stevie Smith, *Selected Poems.* NDP159.
Gary Snyder, *The Back Country.* NDP249.
  Earth House Hold. NDP267.
  Regarding Wave. NDP306.
Enid Starkie, *Arthur Rimbaud.* NDP254.
Stendhal, *Lucien Leuwen.*
  Book I: *The Green Huntsman.* NDP107.
  Book II: *The Telegraph.* NDP108.
Jules Supervielle, *Selected Writings.*† NDP209.
Dylan Thomas, *Adventures in the Skin Trade.*
  NDP183.
  A Child's Christmas in Wales. Gift Edition.
  NDP181.
  Collected Poems 1934-1952. NDP316.
  The Doctor and the Devils. NDP297.
  Portrait of the Artist as a Young Dog.
  NDP51.
  Quite Early One Morning. NDP90.
  Under Milk Wood. NDP73.
Lionel Trilling, *E. M. Forster.* NDP189.
Martin Turnell, *Art of French Fiction.* NDP251.
Paul Valéry, *Selected Writings.*† NDP184
Vernon Watkins, *Selected Poems.* NDP221.
Nathanael West, *Miss Lonelyhearts &
  Day of the Locust.* NDP125.
George F. Whicher, tr.,
  The Goliard Poets.† NDP206.
J. Willett, *Theatre of Bertolt Brecht.* NDP244.
Tennessee Williams, *Hard Candy,* NDP225.
  Camino Real. NDP301.
  Dragon Country. NDP287.
  The Glass Menagerie. NDP218.
  In the Winter of Cities. NDP154.
  One Arm & Other Stories. NDP237.
  The Roman Spring of Mrs. Stone. NDP271.
  27 Wagons Full of Cotton. NDP217.
William Carlos Williams,
  The William Carlos Williams Reader.
  NDP282.
  The Autobiography. NDP223.
  The Build-up. NDP259.
  The Farmers' Daughters. NDP106.
  In the American Grain. NDP53.
  In the Money. NDP240.
  Many Loves. NDP191.
  Paterson. Complete. NDP152.
  Pictures from Brueghel. NDP118.
  The Selected Essays. NDP273.
  Selected Poems. NDP131.
  A Voyage to Pagany. NDP307.
  White Mule. NDP226.
John D. Yohannan,
  Joseph and Potiphar's Wife. NDP262.

Complete descriptive catalog available free on request from
New Directions, 333 Sixth Avenue, New York 10014.   † Bilingual.